DESIGNER'S NOTEBOOK

34

BELVEDERE

Ref-Book 9

CLIP ART   *VARIATION OF LETTERINGS, TITLES & LOGOTYPES*

ARRANGED AND EDITED BY WOLFGANG H. HAGENEY

BELVEDERE

EDITION BELVEDERE CO. LTD., ROME - MILAN (ITALY)

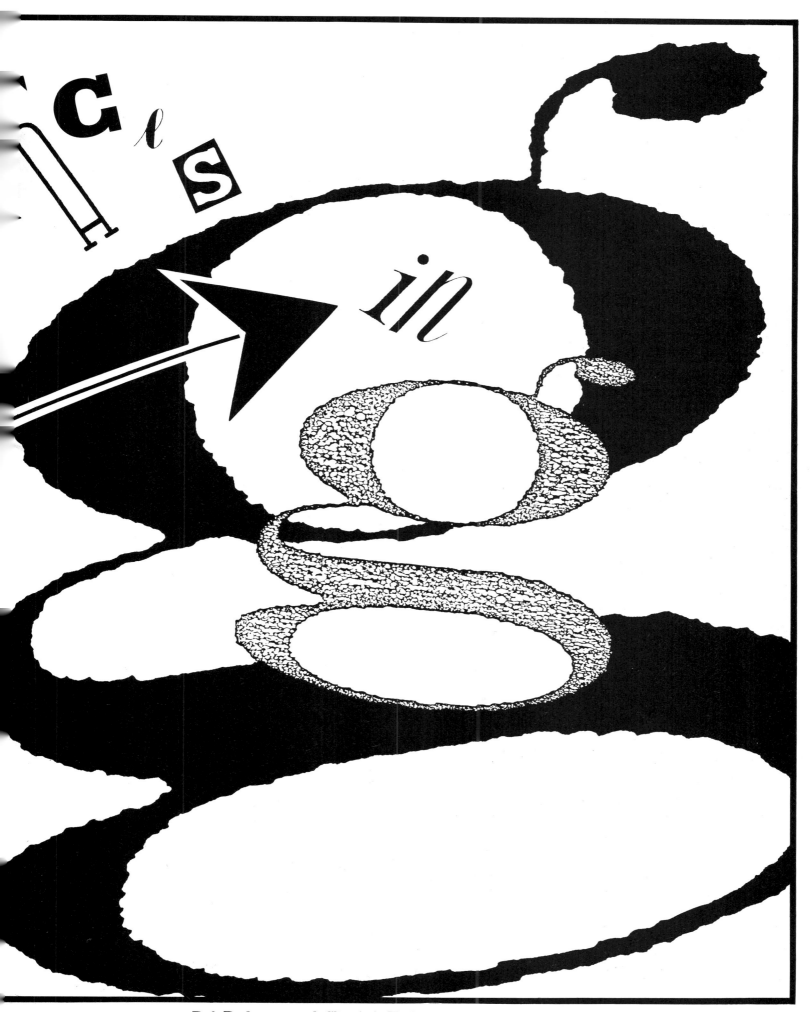

IMPRESSUM

PUBLICATION BY
EDITION BELVEDERE CO. LTD.
ROME-MILAN (ITALY)

© COPYRIGHT 1990
BY EDITION BELVEDERE CO. LTD.

THIS VOLUME WAS FIRST PUBLISHED
IN 1990 (1ST EDITION)

PRINTED IN ITALY BY
STUDIO TIPOGRAFICO, ROME/ITALY
FILMS & PHOTOLITHOGRAPHY BY
BELVEDERE LABORATORIES, ROME/ITALY
LASER TYPE SETTING BY
COMP. LAB. BELVEDERE, ROME/ITALY

LAYOUT & STYLING BY
STUDIO BELVEDERE, ROME/ITALY
EXECUTIVE: ETSUKO KAKUI

ART DIRECTION: HWH & BVR
ARTWORK & GRAPHIC DESIGN BY
STUDIO BELVEDERE, ROME/ITALY

PRINT PRODUCTION: MARCELLO CARMELLINI
STUDIO PRODUCTION: ROSA LENGSFELD
EDITOR & PUBLISHER: WOLFGANG H. HAGENEY

"DESIGNER'S NOTEBOOK" ® is part of the
BELVEDERE PUBLICATIONS INTERNATIONAL
where are also published the
BELVEDERE-DESIGN-BOOKS, DESIGN-BOOKS-
PAPERBACKS, CULTURE DESIGN-BOOKS ®, ARCHI-
BOOKS ®, CAD-BOOKS ®, REF.-BOOKS ®, GRAFIX ®,
PAGE-LAYOUT-SYSTEM ®, IDEA-BOX ®, LOGO-TYPE-
FACES ®, ONE-POINT-BOOKS ®, MIX-MEDIA ®,
CREATIVE SKETCHBOOK ®, IMAGE BANK®
® Registered Trademarks

The BELVEDERE PUBLICATIONS
are available through the general booktrade, art-
supply shops, special agents or exclusively through
the BELVEDERE-DESIGN-CLUB INTERNATIONAL
by international mail order system (for members only)

The publications are also available by subscription or
by standing order directly from the publisher house.
For any information, for membership or subscription,
please write to:

EDITION BELVEDERE CO. LTD.
00196 ROME/ITALY, PIAZZALE FLAMINIO, 19
TEL. (39-6) 360.44.88 / FAX (39-6) 360.29.60
TELEX: 621600 PPRMMZ I-3604488 BELVEDERE

ISBN-88-7070-151-4

EACH SINGLE MOTIF

WYGIWYS

READY TO USE
REAL CLIP-ART
CUT & PASTE
SCAN & PRINT

DESKTOP PUBLISHING

All motifs illustrated and printed in this volume, are ready to use as graphic references and as ideas for visual concepts only. They are useful as a source in the field of everyday-graphic, general art-work, layout or executive graphics. Original Company Logos and Corporate Design are protected by the copyright holders.

It is prohibited to copy, reproduce or transmit designs and motifs for commercial reprints, in any form, by any means, electronic, mechanical, recording or otherwise, or to use the whole concept of this REF.-BOOK issue, without the written permission of the copyright holders. REF.-BOOK® is a registered trademark of Edition Belvedere Co. Ltd. and is copyrighted with all rights reserved.

WHAT YOU GET IS WHAT YOU SEE

INFORMATION ▪▪▪▪▪▪▪▪▪▪▪▪▪▪▪▪▪▪▪▪▪▪▪▪▪▪▪▪█

Letters or their ancestors, ...

the hieroglyphs, are presumably among the most ancient and most cultivated design we can look back on today. A voyage of descovery into the world of scripts is thus not only a journey into the history of design, but also an expedition into various cultural periods. The present book offers an excurtion into the last hundred years, which has attempted to develop scripts corresponding to the various fashions and trends and to give each one of them its own graphic character. The multiplicity of script families, script types and scripts forms and their countless variants, are thus a reflection of the various trends in fashion or design, artistic or stylistic movements to which letters as a means of expressing feeling, but also as a mean of information and communication, have always been subordinated. Energy, power, determination and strength; sensibility, poetry, harmony and grace; movement, dynamism, momentum and peace; quitness, coolness and severity; melodiousness, rhythm, rigidity and elegange: these are just a few of the destinguishing features that characterize the wealth of script types. The present typographical compendium contains hundreds of typefaces and is at your disposal for direct consultation. It will prove extremely helpful in the practical field and in design research. For scripts give access to, and open doors, provide insight into moods and situations. They create atmospheres and new realities. Scripts are a way of typifying and characterizing. They are powerfully expressive and hence very effective as advertising aids.

A real treasure-trove for the commercial artist.

█ ▪▪

TYPEFACES

TYPE

LETTERING

REF. 9

titoli, tipos
escituras
Schrifttypen
types, lettering
logotypes
titles, écritures
typographie
titres, caratteri
characters
logotipi, Titel
tipógrafos
Schriftbilder
caractéres
scritte, titulos

1

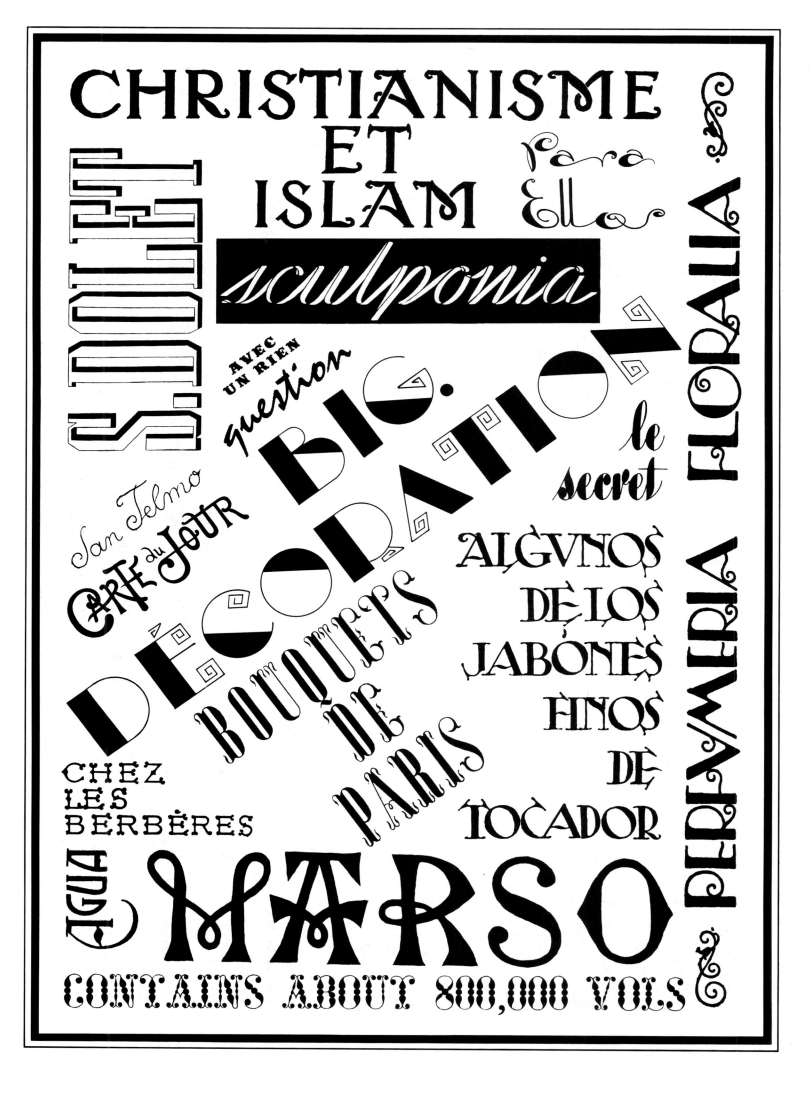

2

PLEIN

Paris

Der Wille

14

VOBACH

WORTH

Eleganza

The better the Fabric

11

FOKKER

ALLEINVERTRIEB

HANSSCHULTZ

HAMBURG-ALSTERDAMM 16-19

Glasfabrik in Schneegattern, O.Oe.

LE THÉÂTRE

JAHRHUNDERTS SEHEN   WIR DIE DRUCK- UND

S. Gryphius, a Printer.

SCHRIFT

3

No!... V'LA ZOLA

De Soto Roma

of New Modes

hotels de ville...

Keeps You Slender!

efo Health Builder

STENDHAL LE REMÈDE

DEMI-GRAS ÉTROIT

aspect romantique 4

de la

DOWN A BACK YARD

by Beverley Nichols

PUBLICITÉ anglaise

Pellicceria

COAL OIL

Allo! BALCONS

SCOTLAND

"RATIONAL" Eva

Land und LEU

Maison Nythis

Mode NU de fijne was
D'IMPRIMERIE weer perfect!

LES EPIS

789 DOG

Des Dieux

Preisausschreiben Wirtschaft

INORGANIQUE

Brillantine COLONIALES
LUSTRALE

CITY

et courtoisie

ACTUALITÉ

5

RAVILIOUS INITIALS

LA CITA

Artemia

A Good

Trois

intérieurs

Artemia

Graffiti

NOCHE

19

"VOL DE NUIT"

NIGHT FLIGHT

femme Scharlachberg

Colortype

CITY

JUMPS

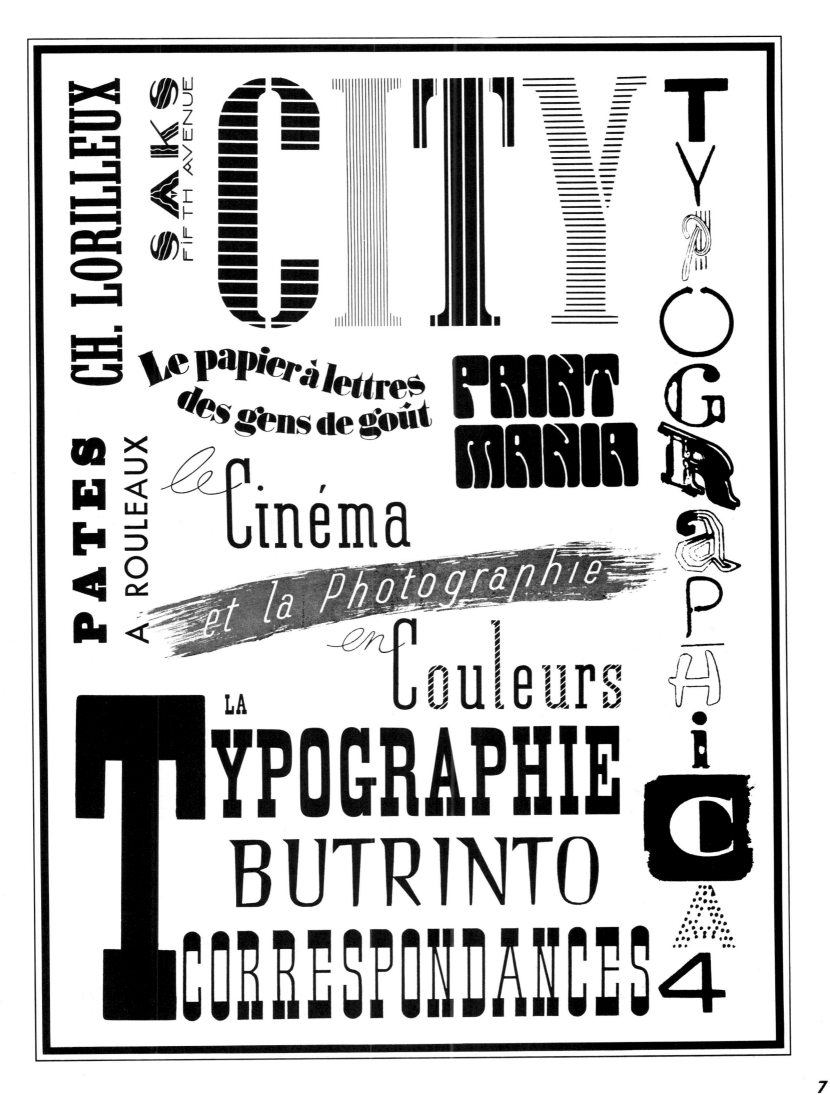

CITY
CH. LORILLEUX
PATES A ROULEAUX
SAKS FIFTH AVENUE
TYPOGRAPHICA 4
Le papier à lettres des gens de goût
PRINT MANIA
le Cinéma et la Photographie en Couleurs
LA TYPOGRAPHIE
BUTRINTO
CORRESPONDANCES

7

JUVENALIEN

Der Meister unter Schülern

ÜBER EIN GEDEIHLICHES LEBEN

STUDENTENHERRSCHAFT

LOTNA

AN DAS GEWISSEN DER WELT

VERBRENNUNGSKOMMANDO

DIE WARSCHAUER "RIVIERA"

ROMANTIK FRAUEN BLUMEN HARLEKIN WARSCHAU

DER MANN DER DREI

URTEILE

BRIEFE AUS BEM OF LA ERZÄHLUNGEN

PERL ELEKTRO TRAKTOR

Sports

HANNO OFFERTO IL VELENO AL RE D'INGHILTERRA

HOWEVER YOU LOOK AT IT

und die reizvollen WILKE-VERSALIEN

GESELLSCHAFT

AUSSTELLUNG

LÜBECKER GENERAL-ANZEIGER

Advances

Voted the Loveliest of

LADIES' HOME JOURNAL

DAS PAPIER FÜR DEN QUALITÄTSDRUCK

KODAKS

CONDANNATO ALL'ITALIA

PER ROMA DIECI IN CONDOTTA

L'ŒUVRE

INTERNATIONAL ADVERTISING ART
MONTHLY MAGAZINE FOR PROMOTING ART IN ADVERTISING

KURHAUS

Ashley

Quosque tan

HANNS ANKER

ZWEITES GESICHT

Balzac

Agua tocado

ÉCHO MODE

TELOS DAS NEUE KLEID

Francesca Ronde

Preis nochmals ermäßigt

der Glaube

GOAL!

Per Salvare Marcello

Green

Gun Car

Allen Trafton

Espagne

Ausgang IM Pelzmantel

Trial Membership

PUISSANCE!

SOURDS...

Cocaína en flor

andern

million, supple

Bundeshauptstadt

THALIA

IDRIZ

VIEIL & NOBLE
CHAMPAGNE
Henri Abelé

Modes d'Enfants
Nº 1.

PARFUMS
LUBIN

Abenteuer

Aufsehen

mettent l'âme
en fête

Château Robert
VICHY

La Meilleure Marque du Monde

MESSERI

HOLLYWOOD

V-ette

Vassarette

KODACHROME

Berthold Wolpe for Bauer

Reklameflächen im Bauentwurf

de Fourrures — Saison 1910/11.

PAPI

INNOVATION

TRADEMARK

This Indenture,

ÉTAIT-CE JULIE?

La Royale Belge

Gemeinde Wien - Städtische Versicherungsanstalt, Landesstelle für Oberösterreich

Specialkonstruktionen

Element Breco's

Colines Rache Flims

BENSIMON

NEGRO CASE Faste

AT LONDON RÉTROGRADE

FABERS Konfession

Mondial

DES LIGNES NOUVELLES

LES POUPÉES

WELT-ANTIQUA

GUTENBERG

FONDERIES DEBERNY PEIGNOT

Where to Shop in London

SACRE

Teppichwebereien

1ST. CIRCULATING LIBRARY, 1725

L E B E D E F F

RECHTSCHREIBBUCH

GENZSCH & HEYSE

MENTZ..1450

LE THÉATRE

Blouses du Matin

COMME IL VOUS PLAIRA

TEAS

IGNORANCE

BIRMINGHAM careful

Newark Advertiser

EACH EVENING

Cambridge News

SPECIAL·

MASQUES

KURZGESCHICHTEN

LATE SPECIAL

Sommersprossen? SHOW

SOMMERKLEIDER AUS
BILLIGEN STOFFEN

DE MEGÈVE

VIAGGO DI NOZZE

DKM

MODERN
BANKING
IS
ELECTRONIC
BANKING

ile
de
FRANCE

FREE LIFE

Zeitlos schön

FREETIME

FEATHERS

TONE

A JACKIE
OLD COYOTE
NOTEBOOK

SMITH.

18

EN TRICOTS EN VACANCES

 TRICOT DE LUXE

W BRAND

 Publicité  NO DISTORTION

 FILM

FLANC BLANC
LE PNEU DE L'ÉLÉGANCE

VXY
D&PABCDEFTUIZ

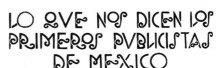 LO QVE NOS DICEN LOS
PRIMEROS PVBLICISTAS
DE MEXICO

THE BOULEVARDS QUADRILLE,

Outline BOLERO

INJUSTEMENT ◆

AU DÉPART L'ATTESA

Meubles
Machines
Methodes

SAG ES MIT ›ELECTROLA‹

JEUX
D'ECHECS

A
ELEGANCIA
E A
ECONOMIA

DON'T YOU DO IT AGAIN or
NO USE AT ME BE WINKING,

KAPEZET RÄDER

LENIEF

MARIPOSAS
NEGRAS...

 LOS TRES CONEJITOS

LA SOFFERENZA VERDE

CHEZ VOTRE COIFFEUR..

SIMPLICIDADE Mein Ferienfenster

Vita brevis Homemaking

MARINE

Chi vuol esser lieto sia!

Celui qu'elle voulait fuir...

1950

Wein!

sposa added but salt—

Applikation

Schwabach

CHIFFONS

mes Cheveux au Vent

Alles

Tüll

EDV

Soieries

millibar

Supalese

QUI SACRIFIER?

De Ventana a Ventana Arkona

hautpflege DANS UN RIDEAU

GABRIELE D'ANNUNZIO

20

Gebr. Klingspor, Offenbach

Alt-Schrift

La Verdad del Esmalte

Christian und Brigitte

Allons vite cacher ces

Fette

Œufs de Pâques

Richtige

DOMANI

Berlin-SW68, Alte Jakobstr. 133

IN DESIGN

IL NEGRO CHE PIANGE

FACE

Innsbruck 5

silenciosamente

DUSKY SKIN

Armorial de la Suisse

Fourey-Galland Chocolatier Paris

Ensign

Muck

LE TRIANGLE

Deutsche Anzeigen

El Hogar y la Moda

Galeries Barbès

KINO

Die Wirtschaftskrise

23

24

Prestige

Zauber-Sprüche

Gegen Ende des 15. und zu Anfang des 16. Jahrhunderts sehen wir die Druck- und Schriftmeister aller Länder in edlem Wetteifer, Schönes und

Gastspielreise des Wiener Burgtheaters

Durchs Land der tausend Seen

Freundschafts Wettspiele 78

Anzeigen - Schrift

a decorative Design by Imre Reiner

Chemische Versuchsanstalt

Oberösterreichischer Verein der Kleinbauern

Donaufahrt

Elektrizitätsgesellschaft, Steyr

PETIT DICTIONNAIRE MÉDICAL *de la semaine*

APRÈS UNE LONGUE NUIT

TOUTE UNE VIE

BRODEZ DES FLEURETTES

Yes, it is a Perfect Plate

LE LOUANGE

· INDEX ·

Les Parfums de FONTANIS

MERRY HOURS

TEPPICHE

UNE LETTRE DU PASSÉ

PAR
MARCELLE AUCLAIR

... CE PETIT AIR

MALERISCHE HÜTE

POLYGONES

POUR EUX

VUIT DE NOËL
QUELQUE PART...

A PROPOS DES „LETTRES DE MON MOULIN"

RESTONS FEMININE

Examinez vos Cheveux

LES COURBES

DEMOTTE

LA BEAUTÉ IMPROVISÉE

UNE SEULE FLEUR
//////
LA PLUS BELLE

House
Beautiful

28

130 Kilo BRUTTO

Frankreichs Militär

BUNDESVERFASSUNG

Die kräftige, moderne Reklameschrift KOLOSS

monotypes

Universität

ZAGORA

Allen Freunden und Bekannten teil

medium and light

AVON

GRAND ARMAGNAC

DE SA MAJESTÉ

CORVINUS bold

NEDERLANDSCHE GEMEENTEWAPENS

LATIN OF

Zehnte Hauptversammlung deutscher Berufsmusiker

Bob, der Alkoholschmuggler

Die Königsberger Akademien

IMPRIMERIE

et du

Prince LIVRE Victor

Taurina

Seul l'Indépendant est le caractère qui
donne toujours satisfaction à vos clients

EN CAMARGUE

TODAY YOUR LIPSTICK

MONT-BLANC

El Amor endulza su flechas

El Hotel Claridge

Orinoka
Fabric

de Paris

ELONGATED

La variedad en los
Sombreros

FRY'S ORNAMENTED

St Etienne

GEBRAUCHSGRAPHIK

MONATSSCHRIFT ZUR FÖRDERUNG KÜNSTLERISCHER REKLAME

ALPHABETICAL TYPOGRAPHY

Woman's Home
Companion

TRA PITTORI
POLEMICHE E CAZZOTTI
ANCHE SCIL⁻IAN HA FIRMATO UNO DEI TROPPI MANIFESTI

Steinfest-
Hose

DÉTAILS

VERTRETER FÜR GROSS-BERLIN
VIKTOR KELETI
CHARLOTTENBURG,
PESTALOZZI-STR. 51

MUSSOLINI NASCOSE A HITLER
la sua arma segreta

Toutes les couleurs

E`venerdi

Schriftgießerei Julius Klinkhardt

¡UNA PLANCHA
ELECTRICA QUE LE
GUSTARA MUCHO!

NOS TRICOTS

Wildunger

Verbrennung

ENTWURF UND AUSFÜHRUNG GANZER WERBEPLÄNE
FÜR DIE GROSSINDUSTRIE, FÜR MITTLERE UND KLEINE BETRIEBE
AUSFÜHRUNG WIRTSCHAFTLICHER UND KULTURELLER
PROPAGANDA ═ ORGANISATION UND BERATUNG

KATALOGE

QUALITÄTSARBEIT

LE SOULIER DE SATIN

Dans la mode

Escales

Radium FAUST

SAKS THINGS SZEN

FIFTH AVENUE

Roma VOC

MODE Le Baron

TRICOTEUSES de Crac

LES MANUSCRITS

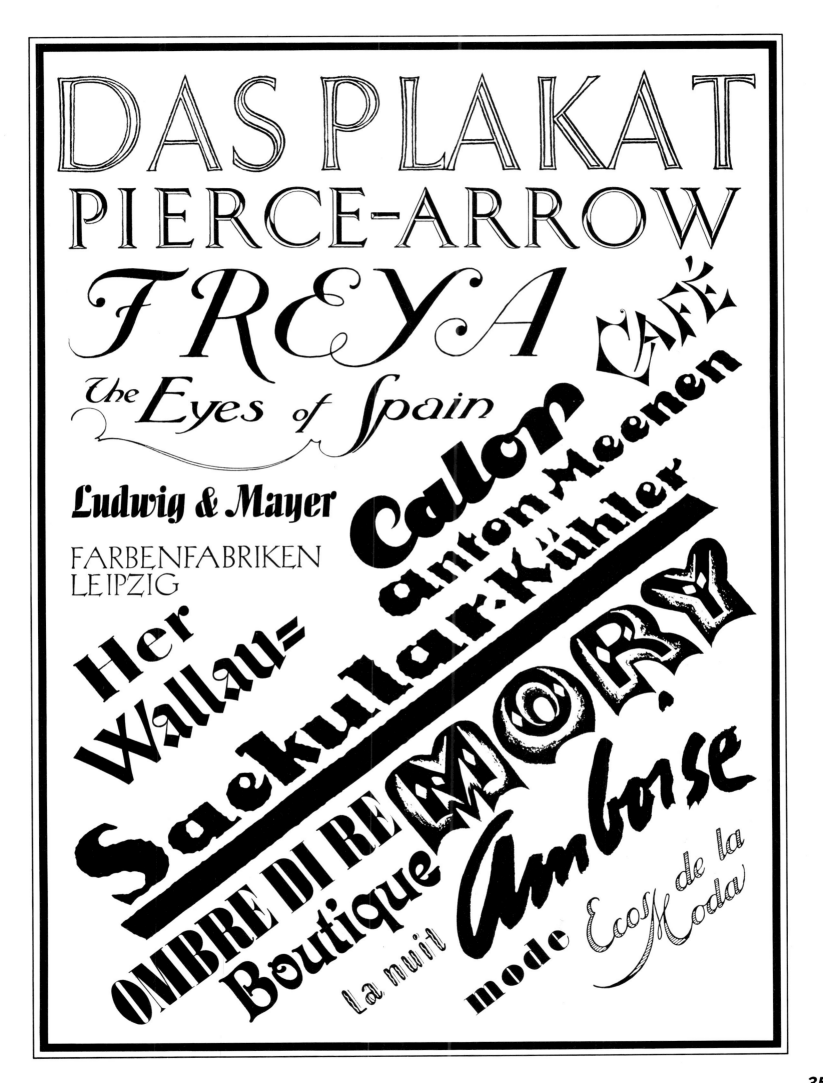

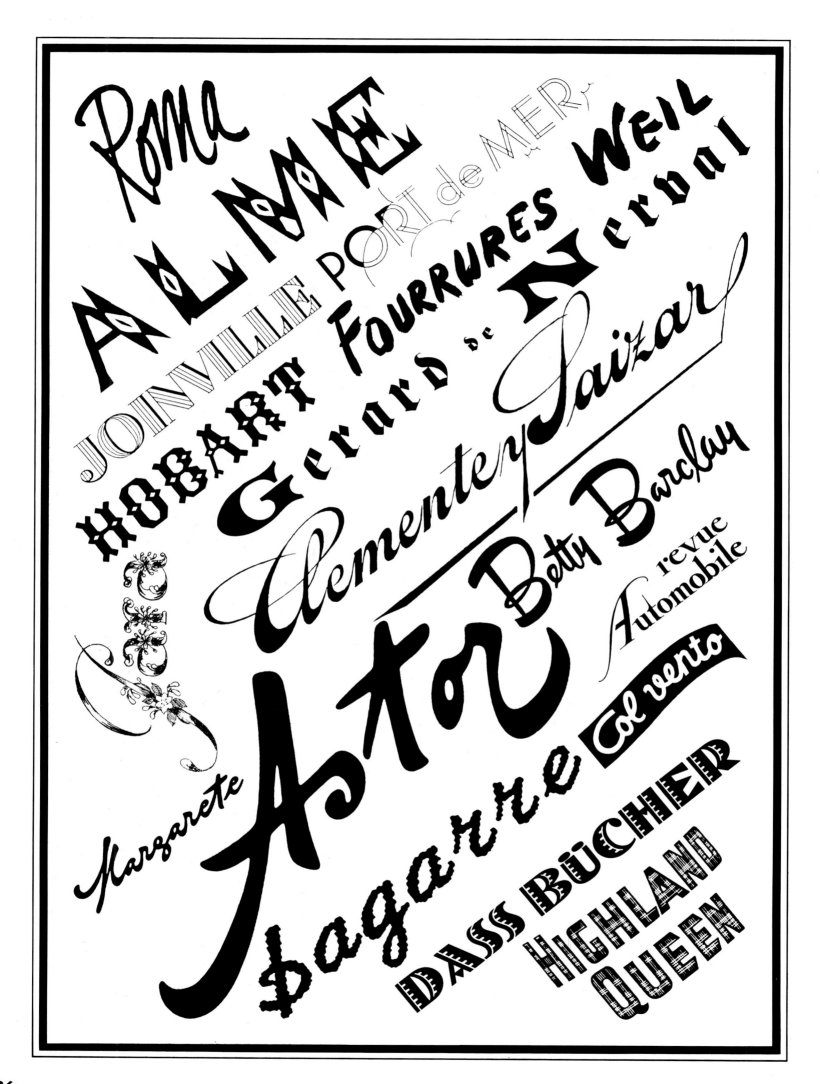

A L'OPÉRA-COMIQUE

Ariane

ans le monde enchanté

des automates

pop Overdrive

rosé problemi SEVILLE

français
doivent savoir

Balle JEUX

MODA

BOUCHE

Wert-
Klischees

Deutsche
Werbegraphik
Values in 1936

New

La
GUERRA
per
L'EUROPA

Quelsque scient
vos goûts...

Die Ausgrabungen aus der Röm

Faire
UN JEU POUR EUX
sera un jeu pour vous

Sonia

Modelling
1939

problemi della casa FÜR

Hosiery Colors for takers

Summer's Varied Moods Holztafeln

je
vieillis
...

HARMONIE

Zeichner Kurzgeschichten

Auf zauberhafte Weise

Wilhelm Woellmer's Schriftgießerei ∗ Messinglinienfabrik ∗ Berlin

Here is Stradivarius from Bauer

1898._ PANORAMA DE TOILETTES DE COMMUNIANTES.._ 1898.

Reichs-
Gartenschau
Dresden
1936

Tictac

(korrekt)

Südamerika-Fahrten

Grand Luxe Parisien ∴ Jupes Parisiennes ∴ Grand
Costumes Trotteur ∴ Album Blouses Nouvelles ∴

MAGQVATER

Grand Album

Sprengstoffkartell

Einladung

Gute Beispiele sagen mehr

LA GRANDE MODE

LA ROSE FRANCE

most famous gifts

Chiquilin

sale del huevo

Verwendungsfähigkeit

39

ACCROCHER LE LE REGARD !

langweilige Kurzgeschichten

Société COOPÉRATIVE

PARIS-ROME

Cycliste Athlétisme Football

PUBLICITÉ

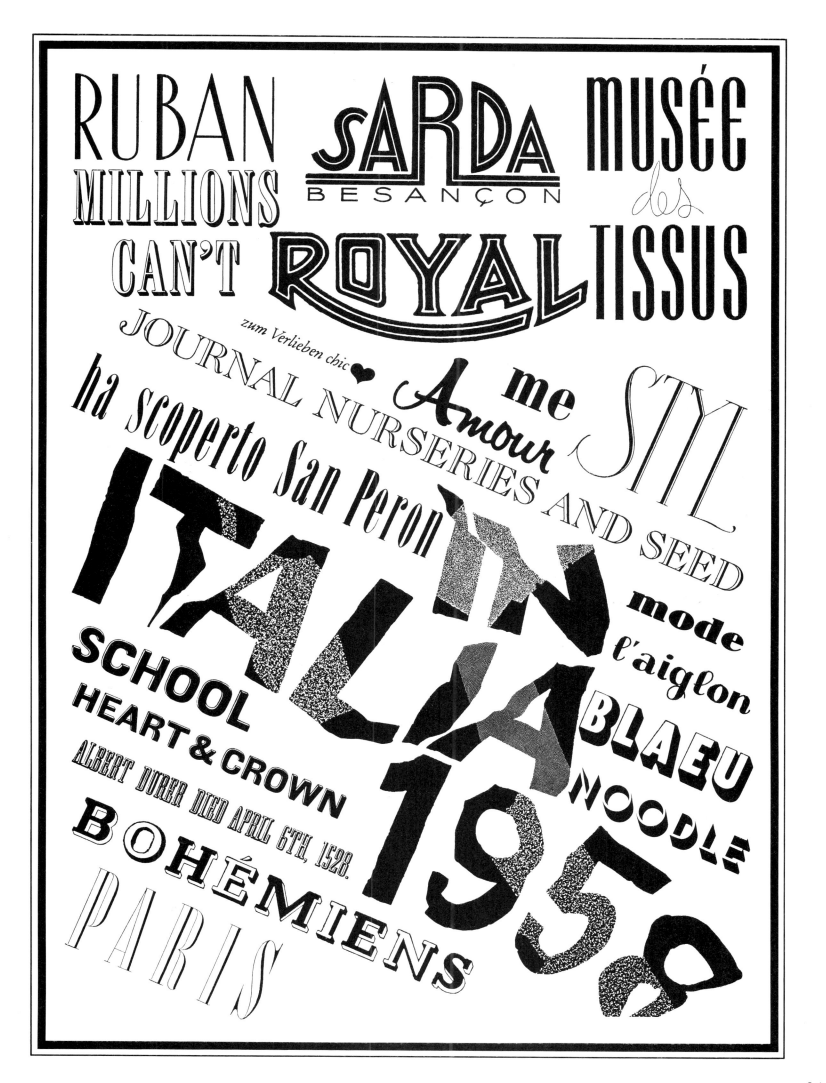

LAIRD MODE

Picture-

ses beffrois, ses

la Création du Monde

PORTOIS & FIX

PYRAMIDE

Wilke-Kursiv

Penrose

Youthline Script

Caumont

Wechselnder

B. Heß Köln

LAMPO

Geschmack

Vogue

ÜBERSEE

Uhu MOZART

Siedlungsbauten in Wels

HOTEL ARLBERGHOF

Darmstadt Meiningen Regensburg Neheim Amsterdam

Eröffnungsfeierlichkeit

GEGEN ENDE DES 15. UND ZU ANFANG DES 16. JAHRHUNDERTS SEHEN WIR DIE DRUCK-
UND SCHRIFTMEISTER ALLER LÄNDER IN EDLEM WETTEIFER, SCHÖNES UND WERTVOLLES

Volksfest in Wels 1932

Die Nerokursiv

Wohlfeile Ganzleinen=Bände der deutschen Klassiker!

A. M. CASSANDRE

AUSTRIAHOF

EHRENURKUNDE

KLEINER ANZEIGER

FONDERIES DEBERNY PEIGNOT

Vereins-Nachrichten

Fonderies DEBERNY PEIGNOT

arum : et deaurauarit wauic·norū

UN CARACTÈRE

Bundesgesetzblatt 59

Fette Secessions-Grotesk :

SIBIRISCHE EDELPELZTIER~FARM

Der Ausdruck des Charakters in der Handschrift

Wege zur Gesunderhaltung und Schönheit für die werktätigen Menschen

»Tizian« die Platte für Porträte

Unsere Obstschädlinge FROSTSPANNER

FONDERIES DEBERNY PEIGNOT

München als Druckstadt

Die herzlichsten Glückwünsche zum Namensfeste!

Bildhauerei EROTIK

PAPAGE

Gebrauchs   graphiker

Kunst zu fahren

5 grosse Blätter

in little two-year-old's mouth!

Two sets of teeth   Werb

BERLIN · POTSDAMERSTR · 103ᴬ · NOLLENDORF 1645 · LÜTZOW

Zweites Jahrbuch der italienischen

JOHN   Werbegraphik ●

MODE

ÖSTERREICHISCHE

FLUGZEUGFABRIK AG

WIENER NEUSTADT

ÖFFAG

KAROSSERIEN

Broschure

SPEZIAL-WERKSTÄTTEN

für Herstellung wetterbeständiger
Stoff-Plakate in allen Grössen
für Aussen-Reklame

GRAS ITALIQUE

LA MARINA E'RIMASTA A GALLA

The Patch Box

As the Season

Genzsch Altona

des jupes

Vanity

Je me mets à votre
franche sur la sorte
vous ramener à Paris

A word
to mothers
on the care
of
baby's bottles

Baruffa
filatore di lana

und

languweilige

Legende

Amortisseurs
Snubbers

sous le manteau
des blouses

& Heyse

Beautiful
Hair—

that reflect the Rainbow

Lanificio Faliero Sarti & Figli

Das ist Quick

13 Roland

Dimitrino
Cigaretten

Spring
freshness—

Five Street Dresses

all winter long
—with asparagus

Reflecting News From Spring Openings

hohlweinbuch Großglock

Egypte Française

Wirtschaft

Schwarz

Weiß

Alltag

ROMAN BOTSCHAFT „Willigs"

Dominique Vous Parle Allo! Différente

ô combien

SON PÈRE Disches

RICAMI
MAGLIERIA
MODA Schönheit UN

& South Yorkshire News

Schríft OFFSETDRUCK

ENTWURF Description

ALBERT PFISTER'S Unter Null Grad

KLEINAUTO- UND MOTOREN-WERKE

51

52

Cyko India Iris-Seife

12MO BOOK

2 Years

REFLETS

BOUTIQUES

À

SORTILÈGES

MERRY HOURS

VIVRE

EST

UN ART

JOHN J. ASTOR

TROIS VALSES

A DONATUS

JAEGER-LECOULTRE

La parola alla SCIENZA

La marina da Guerra 481 ricostruita

HÔTELS
TRANSPORTS
bagages
PLAGES

Gay Top

The pick of America's

Unsere Kirche
Evangelisches Gemeindeblatt
Herausgegeben vom Evangelischen Preßverband für Schlesien

Offerte mittelst Filmbildes

STRUB

FARBENLIEFERANTEN: Anden
BERGER & WIRTH

SONNE auf MACEDONIEN

MANY NIFTY MAXIMS LOWER LAZY TYPESETTER'S...

CORISIA in Oberösterreich

Ausdrucksmöglichkeiten

"the Hundred Million"

WOOD-MILNE

NAVIGAZIONE

KÍKIRIKI
SECCION·ESPECIAL·PARA·NIÑOS

Spamer Leipzig
Deutschlands größte
Industrie- und Werkdruckerei

JEZLER
ECHT SILBER

Chio Chips

"THE DURABLE"

NOVITÀ MUSICALI

Photogravure Process by Clarke & Sherwell Ltd.

MERIT!

BAGATELLEN

BAR

Doppel herz

Dicen que...

E

L'APOCALISSE

PER MORIR...

Modisteria casera

MARTINE

Unifinix Today

Riccione

Porte-Plume
(Ideal)
Waterman

KUNSTDRUCK-U. VERLAGSANSTALT **WEZEL & NAUMANN** A.G. LEIPZIG

KÜNSTLER-PLAKATE, DAUERKALENDER, FALTSCHACHTELN

LETZTE WIRKSAME REKLAME-NEUHEITEN: **IMIT. WASSERSPIELE** KOSTENLOS MIT ARBEITEND

NEUE LANDKARTEN REKLAMETEXT

Restlos

vollkommen · rauchlos

DER KAMPF CHE

È RIBASSATO SPARKASSE
ALLGEMEINE

L'ESTONIA MODERNA

FRANK·HAVILAND
60 FAUBOURG POISSONNIÈRE PARIS

Le Grand Tailleur
Robes d'Intérieur

IL LIBRO
DEL GIORNO

Holla the superb script letter
designed by *Rudolf Koch*

LA BEAUTÉ POUR TOUTES

AFFARE und mit jedem
Betriebsstoff

BERLIN W 35 LÜTZOWSTR · 102 · 4

la mode
des tailleurs
simple et pratique
à Paris

Consigli e ricette per la cucina dei piccoli

Fulgurantes

Vu à
Auteuil

Rythmes

Collections

Tendances nouvelles

Ava
Gardner

quelques
blouses

Première Soirée

d'Hiver

le tailleur de Guerre

63

64

DEVAMBEZ

Baumaterialien-Handlung

CHRISTIAN BÉRARD

Amtsdirektion

ACTUALITÉ

Der deutsche Großsender in Königswusterhausen

Städtisches Freibad

Mannheim

Neueste Schriften-Garnituren für Zeitun

PRIMAVERA A S. MORITZ

Regensburg 13

Neustadt Wiener

Richard Wagners Werke

EIN KLASSIKER

Magistrat der Landeshauptstadt Linz

FARBENFABRIK A.LEINER

Adriana Castelli Cutuli

FAHRPLAN

Salamanders and Graphic Arts

Die zarte Kartenschrift Mirabelle

HISTOIRE ET DÉCORATION

ILLUSTRATION

Ausstellung des Oberösterreichischen Kunstvereines

JAGUARS AND MOTORSHOWS

Reichsverein der österreichischen Kunstgewerbler

Krone ÖLE

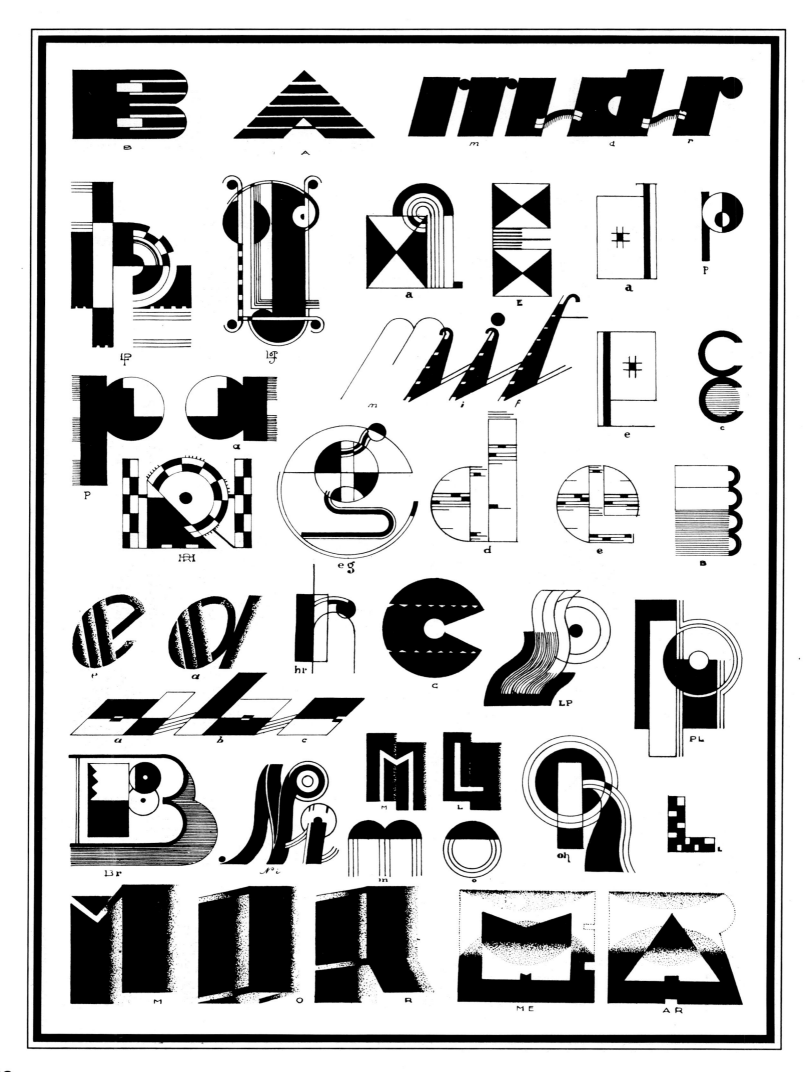

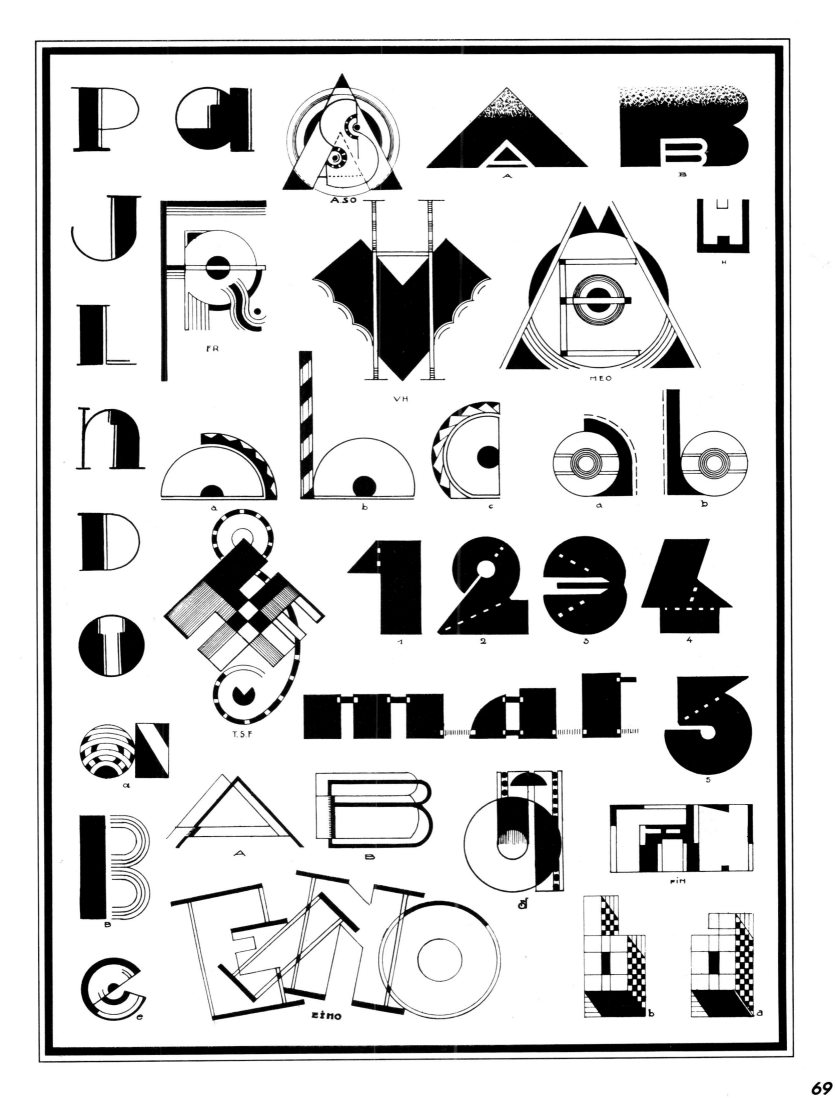

NEW YORK ROMANCE

PER SCONFIGGERE LA CELLULITE

LES CHÂTEAUX DE LA LOIRE

AUSTELLUNG MODELL-HUT

DER SCHEUE MARONI-BRATER

latino matematica

SOMBRERO

È attivata una borsa nuova in città.

FORMAGGIO BEL PAESE

Die Einkaufsstelle für jeden Papierbedarf

WE ARE PROUD TO WORK

TEMPEST TITLING

Wachauer Stube

A CALIPH OF CORDOVA,

Die Donau von Ulm bis Wien

NORDDEUTSCHE SCHIFFAHRTS-GES.

ORANGEN-SAFT

These taste much better

Friedrichswald

Neue halbfette römische Antiqua

MODERNE TYPEN

Wilhelm Woellmer's Schriftgießerei

Fonderies DEBERNY PEIGNOT

Elementarereignisse

LITHOGRAPHISCHE KUNSTANSTALT GEORG REISSL

AFFICHES

Vereinsnachrichten

technisch vollkommen, nach Entwürfen erster

Gasinstallation

Not Her MIDNIGHT EYES

Romane FOTOGRAFA

Published by Alec Tiranti, London 1952   ENGLISH ROMANESQUE SCULPTURE

Deutschland

HANS LANDSBERGER - BERLIN S.

DER OLYMPIONIKE

lebendige Kraft

ÖSTERREICHISCHER REKLAME-FACHLEUTE, GEBRAUCHSGRAPHIKER

Schreibmaschinen

Cream Buns

An die 500.000 Hausfrauen, die sich den Bosch-Kühlschrank nur zum Butterkühlen wünschen

Schmalfette

Rector Magnifice

Goodrich

CHAMPAGNE

Conversation

Se raser...

Ce Bonheur

Vorausfetzung für ihre

LEADERSHIP

RUDOLPH HERTZOG

Monarchie oder Republik?

Vita brevis

Tricotons...

Overland

DE

Victoria and Albert Museum

JOHN SINCLAIR

Vergängliche

Laura Scudders

COMTESSE DE TONNERRE

Unfere Neuheiten

HOEHL

CHIROMANZIA DEI MURI

ars longa

Pasta

Tricots légers

GORDON'S DRY GIN

POUR

la chaleur

Album Jeunesse Parisienne
Grand Album de Chapeaux

spricht für sich—

SCHÖNES UND WERTVOLLES

„WIENER CHIC" IST DAS TONANGEBENDE FACHBLATT

MANI DI FATA

DAS MODE=JOURNAL

BIANCHINI FÉRIER

Mode Bericht

La Couturière Parisienne

N° 63.

Rundschau in Kärnten

Donau Werbedienst

Hautes Nouveautés pour Mode et Couture

Ariès

Die Kultur der Reklame

ist unbegrenzt!

Internationales Droste

Qualität

Müller

Pettinatura "alla Moda"

vuol dire

pettinatura "Tricofilina"

Zeit ist

SOMMERFAHRPLAN

Werben Sie neue Plakatfreunde

Tannenberg

Ich erkläre hierdurch
meinen Beitritt zum Verein der Plakatfreunde e.V.
für Kunst und Kultur in der Reklame.

cumillo &ille mecum. Juumpe
lyx eqt illu animu quue uitumpuam

Typographie

Die neue Probe der Deutschland-Schriften ist ein

Beweis hierfür; sie ist vorbildlich wie die Schriften, die sie zeigt:

Verein der Plakatfreunde e.V.
in
Charlottenburg 2

Alles

Delphin

Kantstraße 158

der Wallau

Der Bibel erster
Band
Israel
und Juda

„Großdeutsch"

wird auf einen Blick gelesen!

Weinbau

Charles Packer & Co Ltd.
GOLDSMITHS & SILVERSMITHS

Pliofilm *

Berliner Buchbinderei
Wübben und Co
Berlin SW 68, Kochstr. 60/61

Erlebensversicherung

OPENED FREE IN 1701.

WALDORF ASTORIA

GRAHAM-PAIGE

Weiß-und

Derby

UTIS

Schriftgießerei

GEGEN ENDE DES

DEBERNY

et

PEIGNOT

Wirkwaren

Gewährung von Rechtsschutz für die Mitglieder

TORERO

Hélios

Funke

DUELLO

LYON

Allgemeines öffentliches Krankenhaus

VENISE

Le raccommodeur de cathédrales

HABITAT

COLONIAL

CORROSION

Marlboro Cigarette for Those Who Can Afford 20¢ for the Best

MISSIONNAIRE ET RELIGIEUX

Ricil's

Décor pour un Ballet 4

Taschenkalender

GEMEINDEVERTRETER

JOINVILLE

Schwimm- und Rudersportartikel

FRY, 1799

La Coiffure

Des Lebens Sinn

Rythme et Danse

Reisen und

BELGIQUE

la

LUXEMBOURGEOISE

Aigua de Colonia Añeja

LA MODE FRANÇAISE

Ultra

Unser großer Meister

No!..

Bon Marché

WE
AGAIN EMPHASISE
THE MERITS OF
EXCELSIOR ART

Dante

CAPRICE

Bodoni

a lovely time

Gegen Ende des 15.

for reflection

MENU

ist nur ein Gleichniß,

Du Moulin de Daudet à Fontvielle

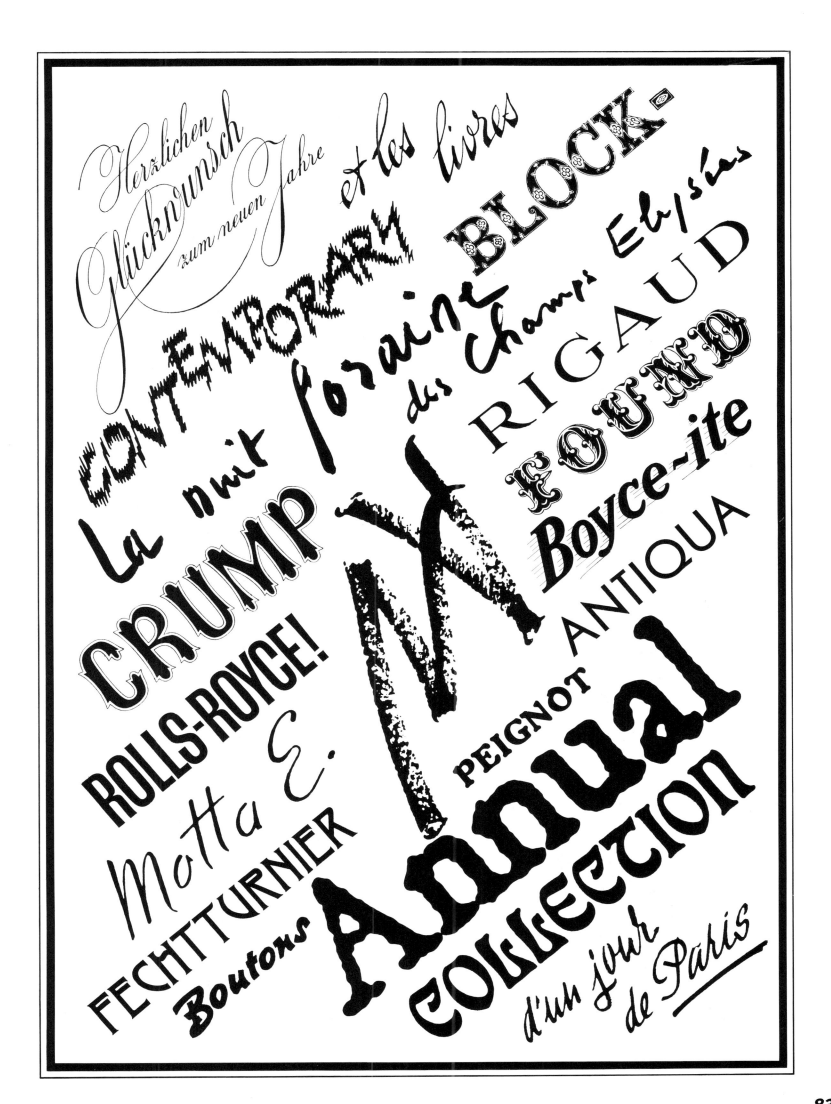

83

84

This design by George Trump is a great improvemen

climatici

FIORITA DI LAVANDA
SOFFIENTINI

TI·CLAVDIVS·CAESAR·AVGVSTVS
GERMANNICVS·PONTIFEX·MAXIM

GRAPHIQUE

increased production

Thés

RESTAURANTS

cabarets

DANCINGS

SPECTACLES

divers

etc..

BUGATTI

CIENTE
NON SEMBRA MA CI SONO

in gleicher Klarheit

DES
FRONCES
QUI SE FONT
ELLES-MÊMES

ROJO CLARO
ROJO GERANIO
ROJO ELÉCTRICO

Aufforstung

Morris "Snap-Open" Pack

Suggests

Carica politica

bei allen Tourenzahlen

Le Crochet

Ha VOLUTO SALVARLA

O HANARRO DANNORICIS F

suite

Cégéto

LAIT de COLOGNE

Chris-Craft

O'ROSSEN

Typophily in Summer County

SOLE D'EGITTO

TEELA-WOOKET

lavez-vous

VOYAGES & SPORTS

E POCHE NAVI
LE PATRON BELL

Soir de Paris

IL SOFA

LA VILLE

George Washington

VOTRE
JARDIN EST
UN TRÉSOR

GARDEZ-EN LES FRUITS
AVEC SOIN

IL CAPITANO NASCA   PRIMAVERA DI SANGUE

There's something better to eat

Side Shops of New York

ACTUALITÉ GRAPHIQUE

La vezzosa

L'Elégance
DES LIGNES

Disfrute

Novità per le signore eleganti!.

A vaillans

♡ riens

il était un petit enfant

LA
FEMME
IDEALE

Keyboard

La gaine

Alle Damen
lieben und bevorzugen

Agfa

Strümpfe und
Unterwäsche

LA MODE AU MICROSCOPE

le côté subjectif

Per il vostro corredo!

1900

Vergänglich

filiforme

vitamines

Trois esprits

SPORT qualitätsware

in einer alten Firma!...

always healthy hair!

heller Klang

Aha!

und neue Farbigkeit

Rezept!

Beleuchtung

Hamburg
Verkehrsreklamen
Anschlagsäulen
Hoenicke & Kypke

Aurek-Gesellschaft

für Schaufenster,
Strassenbahn- u.-
Eisenbahn-
Reklame

Lucien says... Lelong

DECURION SIGISMUNDO

Krankenhilfe

Allerlei

Cegeka
Vexillum
Amor
ALBOGEN
cremata
ALBINA
Silver Leaf
Thomas A Edison
Savonine.
WIHA
Wilhelm Bartels

BLENAL Salome
Gliolin
EUPURGO

94

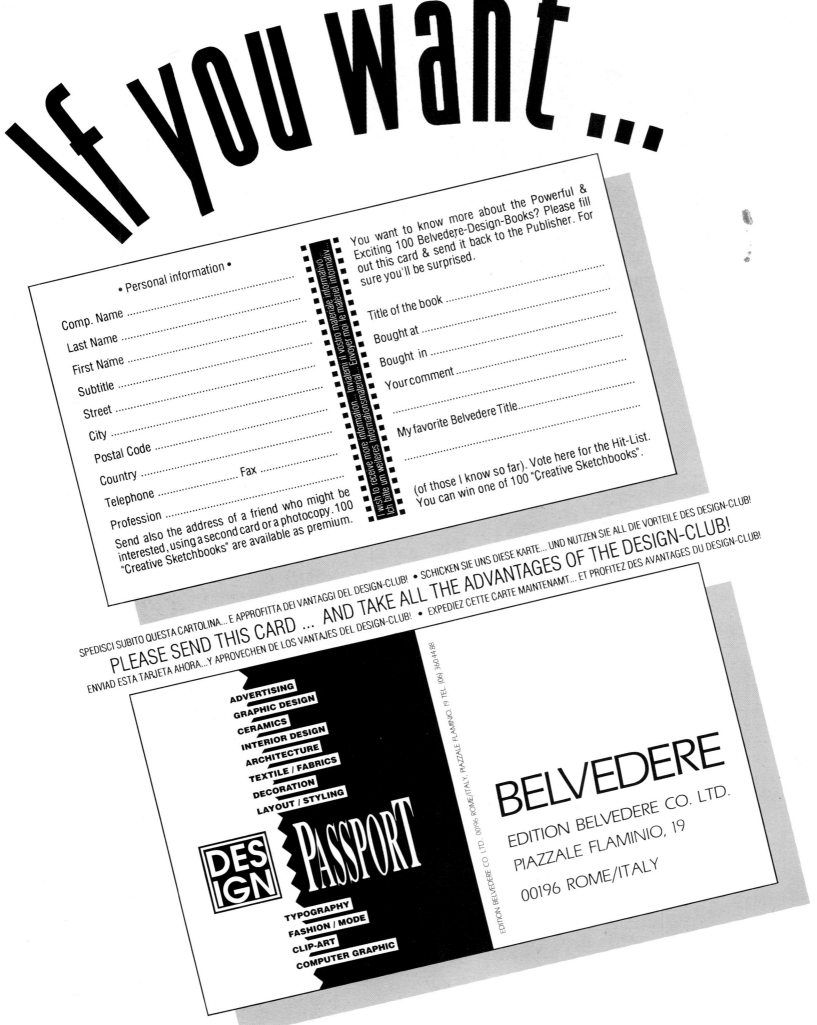

Good Design Books are hard to find. It takes you time and money to get the right images & references you need for your work. But now you can have it all more easily. Choose simply the best in its field: Belvedere-Design-Books, "made in Italy". Go, and ask for the DESIGN-CLUB INTERNATIONAL, and you will get a special offer (free of charge) immediately. It will surprise you.

E' difficile trovare buoni libri di design. Ci vuole tempo e denaro per avere le immagini e le idee giuste. Ma adesso é tutto piú facile. Scegliete solamente il meglio: i Belvedere-Design-Books, "made in Italy". Chiedete del DESIGN-CLUB INTERNATIONAL e avrete subito gratis delle offerte eccezionali che vi sorprenderanno.

Gute Designbücher sind schwierig zu finden. Es erfordert oft viel Zeit und Geld, um an die richtigen Ideen & Vorlagen zu gelangen. Doch jetzt ist alles viel leichter. Wählen Sie einfach das Beste: Belvedere-Design-Books, "made in Italy". Erkundingen Sie sich nach dem DESIGN-CLUB INTERNATIONAL und Sie werden unverzüglich & kostenlos ein Spezial-Angebot erhalten, das Sie überraschen wird.

Es realmente difícil encontrar buenos libros de design. Se necesitan tiempo y dinero para obtener las imágenes & ideas apropiadas para vuestro trabajo. Ahora todo es más facil. Puede conseguirse lo mejor con los Belvedere-Design-Books, "made in Italy". Es suficiente solicitarlos al DESIGN-CLUB INTERNATIONAL; inmediatamente, y gratis, recibiréis meravillosas ofertas.

Il n'est pas facile de trouver de bons ouvrages de design. Vous avez sans doute souvent perdu beaucoup de temps et d'argent dans la recherche d'images & d'idées nouvelles. Aujourd'hui cela vous sera plus facile. Choisissez toujours le meilleur: les Belvedere-Design-Books, "made in Italy". Écrivez au DESIGN-CLUB INTERNATIONAL et vous recevrez gratis, et par retour du corrier une offre spéciale qui vous surprendra agréablement.

GRAPHICOLOR
300 GRAPHICAL MOTIFS WITH FANTASY ALL IN COLOR

BELVEDERE

ATLANTIS

BELVEDERE

MEMORY
LACE DESIGNS - A VERSION OF TEXTILE DECORATION FROM 1920-1930

BELVEDERE

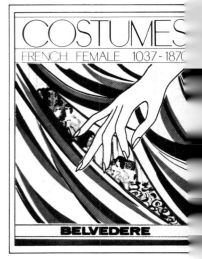

COSTUMES
FRENCH FEMALE 1037 - 1870

BELVEDERE

C·O·M·P·U·T·E·R
1 2 3
GRAPHIC

BELVEDERE

PARIS
1928-1929

BELVEDERE

Floral Art

BELVEDERE

SUITE
No. 35

BELVEDERE

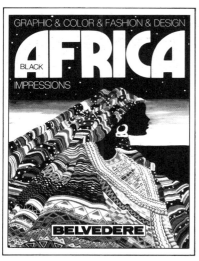

GRAPHIC & COLOR & FASHION & DESIGN

AFRICA
BLACK
IMPRESSIONS

BELVEDERE

DECOR

BELVEDERE

MODE & SPORT

BELVEDERE

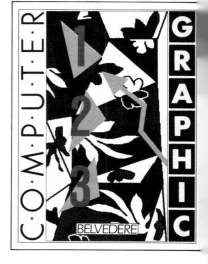

C·O·M·P·U·T·E·R
1 2 3
GRAPHIC

BELVEDERE

ORNAMENT

BELVEDERE

FLORAL
DREAM

BELVEDERE

JAPAN
IDEABOOK

BELVEDERE

PAGE LAYOUT
TYPEFACES IN COMPOSITIONS

ONLY
THE
BEST
1980
1990

BELVEDERE

Oriental flowers
BELVEDERE

BELVEDERE
PHOTO-FASHION

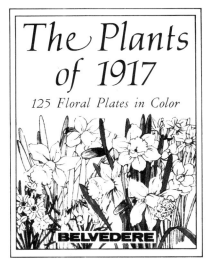

The Plants of 1917
125 Floral Plates in Color
BELVEDERE

RACES · CULTURES · ARTIFACTS · COSTUMES · ORNAMENTS
ETHNO GRAPHIC
BELVEDERE

Bouquets
BELVEDERE

DESIGN BOOKS
BELVEDERE

COLOR symphony
BELVEDERE

TEXTILE PATTERNBOOK
BELVEDERE

TARTANS
BELVEDERE

GRAPHIC - DESIGNS
RHYTH MUSIC
LINES & STRIPES IN VARIATIONS
FOR TEXTILE & DECORATION
BELVEDERE

REPERTOIRE
MODERN INTERIOR DESIGN
1928 - 1929
BELVEDERE

GRAPHIC FLOWER
BELVEDERE

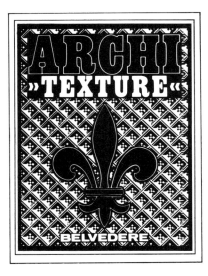

ARCHI "TEXTURE"
BELVEDERE

FRESCO
BELVEDERE

AUTOMOBILE 1920 1940
BELVEDERE

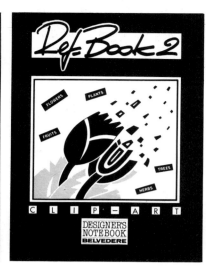

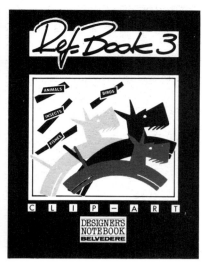

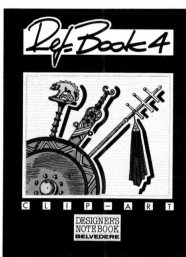

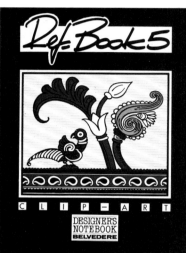

REF-BOOKS" SERVE THE COMMERCIAL OR INDUSTRIAL ARTIST AS A STOREHOUSE OF ALWAYS NEW IDEAS AND MODELS. THEY FORM A WORKING INSTRUMENT AND REFERENCE WORK FOR "EVERYDAY GRAPHICS" AND OFFER WIDE-RANGING APPLICATIONS AS A CONSULTIVE TOOL IN THE FIELD OF VISUAL COMMUNICATION. REF-BOOKS" OFFER YOU MANY THOUSAND SINGLE MOTIFS WHICH ARE AT YOUR DISPOSAL FOR YOUR OWN INDIVIDUAL USE, ALL COPYRIGHT-FREE.

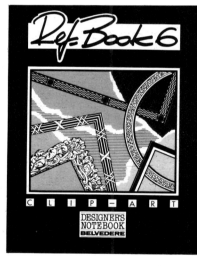

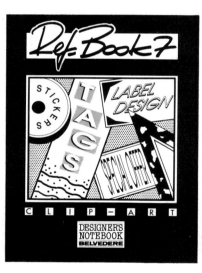

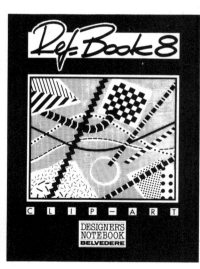

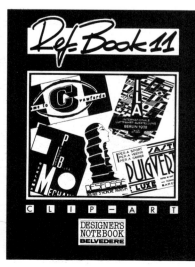

MODE 1938

DESIGNER'S NOTEBOOK BELVEDERE

KIMONO

DESIGNER'S NOTEBOOK BELVEDERE

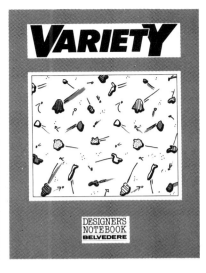

VARIETY

DESIGNER'S NOTEBOOK

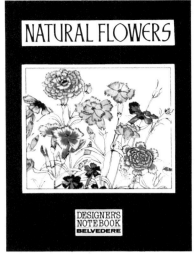

NATURAL FLOWERS

DESIGNER'S NOTEBOOK BELVEDERE

FLOREAL

DESIGNER'S NOTEBOOK BELVEDERE

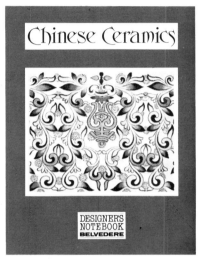

Chinese Ceramics

DESIGNER'S NOTEBOOK BELVEDERE

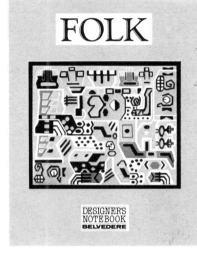

FOLK

DESIGNER'S NOTEBOOK BELVEDERE

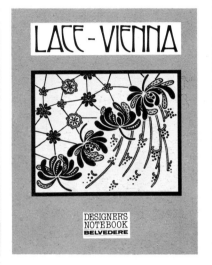

LACE - VIENNA

DESIGNER'S NOTEBOOK BELVEDERE

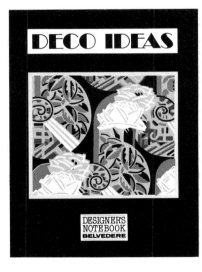

DECO IDEAS

DESIGNER'S NOTEBOOK BELVEDERE

TRANS FIGURATION

DESIGNER'S NOTEBOOK BELVEDERE

MODE 1924

DESIGNER'S NOTEBOOK BELVEDERE

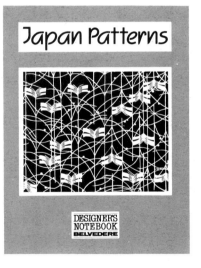

Japan Patterns

DESIGNER'S NOTEBOOK BELVEDERE

Textures

DESIGNER'S NOTEBOOK BELVEDERE

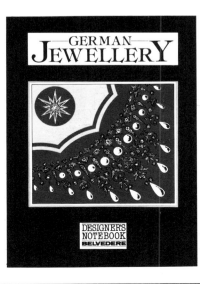

GERMAN **JEWELLERY**

DESIGNER'S NOTEBOOK BELVEDERE

MELANCHOLY

DESIGNER'S NOTEBOOK BELVEDERE

DESIGN & LIGHT

DESIGNER'S NOTEBOOK BELVEDERE

PARIS
VOL. 1 · 1928
BELVEDERE

PARIS
VOL. 2 · 1929
BELVEDERE

AFRICA
VOL. 1
BELVEDERE

AFRICA
VOL. 2
BELVEDERE

GRAPHIC FLOWER
VOL. 1
BELVEDERE

GRAPHIC FLOWER
VOL. 2
BELVEDERE

FRESCO
VOL. 1
BELVEDERE

FRESCO
VOL. 2
BELVEDERE

DECORATIVE ORNAMENT
VOL. 1
BELVEDERE

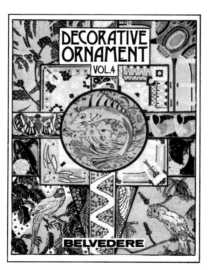

DECORATIVE ORNAMENT
VOL. 4
BELVEDERE

ETHNO GRAPHIC 1
BELVEDERE

ETHNO GRAPHIC 4
BELVEDERE

Floral Art 1
BELVEDERE

Floral Art 3
BELVEDERE

GRAPHICOLOR
300 GRAPHICAL MOTIFS WITH FANTASY ALL IN COLOR
VOL. 1
BELVEDERE

GRAPHICOLOR
300 GRAPHICAL MOTIFS WITH FANTASY ALL IN COLOR
VOL. 2
BELVEDERE

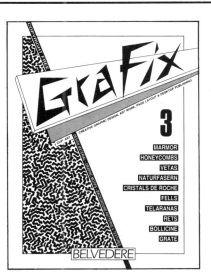

THIS SERIES PLACES IN THE HANDS OF THE COMMERCIAL ARTIST AN INVALUABLE CORPUS OF DESIGN MATERIAL THAT IS BOTH FAST IN APPLICATION AND HIGHLY TOPICAL. THOUGH PREDOMINANTLY TIMELESS AND NEUTRAL, IT DOES NOT LEAVE FASHIONABLE TRENDS OUT OF CONSIDERATION. THE INDIVIDUAL PLATES OF EACH VOLUME PROVIDE THE USER WITH EXTREMELY PRACTICAL AND FULLY REPRODUCIBLE WORKING MODELS. THE NUMBERED MOTIFS ARE AT HIS IMMEDIATE DISPOSAL, AND CAN BE USED WITHOUT PROBLEM, IN THE DIRECT WAY ACCORDING TO THE CUT AND PASTE, SCANN AND PRINT METHODS AS BASIC GRAPHIC MATERIAL. CLIP-ART MEANS UP-TO-DATE AND CONTINUOUSLY NEW STIMULI, NEW SUGGESTIONS, WHICH CAN BE USED FOR EVERY TYPE OF CREATIVE DESIGN. AN ONGOING SERIES WHICH WILL BE SUPPLEMENTED WITH NEW PATTERNS AND IDEAS ON A PERMANENT BASIS. CLIP-ART MOTIFS ARE ABSOLUTLY COPYRIGHT-FREE.

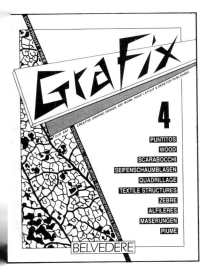
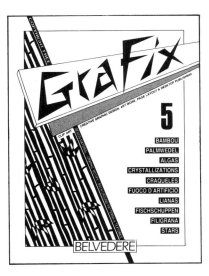

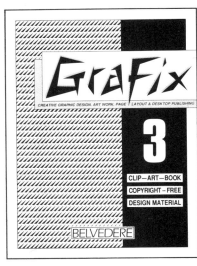

PUBBLICITÀ